100 ways to Rebuild the world™

Written by
Helen Murray

DK

Contents

Introduction p8

What will you do today? p10

1 Offer a hug p12
2 Pick up a friendship p12
3 Boost positivity p13
4 Ready, steady, grow... p14
5 Get moving! p15
6 Give a thank-you card p15
7 Save your pennies p16
8 Make someone laugh p16
9 Be animal aware p17
10 Become a tidying whizz p18
11 Celebrate differences p19
12 Be a litter champion p20
13 Share your skills p20
14 Eat a rainbow p21
15 Create a family game p22
16 Talk to the new kid p23
17 Be a food-waste hero p24
18 3, 2, 1... run! p25
19 Go on a bug hunt p26
20 Give toys a new home p28
21 Discover your history p29
22 Love yourself p30

23 Sing for joy p30
24 Host an awards night p31
25 Go on a pet adventure p32
26 Share it! p33
27 Be kind online p33
28 Top a chore chart p34
29 Bring the birthday joy p35
30 Help a classmate p36
31 Offer your seat p36
32 Start a chain of creativity p37
33 Say cheese! p38
34 Be the news p39
35 Lights out p40
36 Solve it! p41
37 Bee friendly p42
38 Welcome everyone p43
39 Have your say p43
40 Step into their shoes p44
41 Be brave p45
42 Swap it! p45
43 Make your school sparkle p46
44 Be a chef p47
45 Celebrate you! p48
46 Hunt for rainbows p49
47 Become a team player p50
48 Borrow kindly p51
49 Turn off the tap p51

50 Tell a LEGO® tale p52
51 Be awesome and recycle p53
52 Make someone feel great p54
53 Unplug it! p54
54 Celebrate where you live p55
55 Go bird-watching p56
56 Look on the bright side p57
57 Befriend an elderly person p58
58 Have sweet dreams p58
59 Be fair! p59
60 Start a club p60
61 Surprise a pal p60
62 Celebrate heroes p61
63 Build together p62
64 Host a book swap p63
65 Stand up for what's right p64
66 Thank your teacher p65
67 Be a good neighbour p66
68 Say no to rubbish p66
69 Start a worm farm p67
70 Be their biggest fan p68
71 Wish them well p69
72 Respect the rules p70
73 Focus your mind p71
74 Be kind, tidy! p71
75 Start a "library of things" p72
76 Be a kindness detective p72

77 Get outdoors! p73
78 Treat someone p74
79 Grow vegetables p75
80 Read all about it! p75
81 Listen to others p76
82 Volunteer at school p76
83 Give a thoughtful gift p77
84 Meet new critters p78
85 Start a special book club p79
86 Buy local p79
87 Explore the world p80
88 Give a helping hand p81
89 Save paper p82
90 Celebrate the little things p82
91 Be kind to yourself p83
92 Do something you love
    every day p84
93 Plant a butterfly paradise p85
94 And breeeeathe! p85
95 Be kind to furry friends p86
96 Take a shower challenge p87
97 Look around you! p87
98 Create a "tower of change" p88
99 Spread some cheer p89
100 Over to you! p89
    Checklist p90
    Acknowledgements p92

Introduction

Be inspired to make a difference to the world around you – all while getting creative with your LEGO® bricks! Even the smallest changes and acts of kindness can make a big difference.

Discover 100 different ways to be brave, curious, and kind – to yourself, to others, to your community, and to the planet. You can read the book from cover to cover, dip in for ideas, or even see if you can complete the checklist on page 90. Grab your LEGO bricks and get inspired to make the world an even more awesome place to live!

THINK BIG... BUT START SMALL!

What will you do today?

It can be hard to know where to begin to rebuild the world! Here are a few questions you can ask yourself to get started. What are you waiting for?

A friend

Bring a smile to a pal's face with one of the following: **8** Make someone laugh (p16); **40** Step into their shoes (p44); **70** Be their biggest fan (p68).

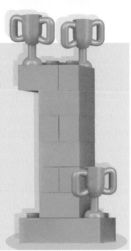

Who needs some love today?

My family
Surprise them with one of these: **78** Treat someone (p74); **24** Host an awards night (p31); **83** Give a thoughtful gift (p77).

A neighbour
Make someone's day: **6** Give a thank-you card (p15); **67** Be a good neighbour (p66); **99** Spread some cheer (p89).

A classmate
Reach out to someone in your class: **13** Share your skills (p20); **30** Help a classmate (p36); **38** Welcome everyone (p43).

Where shall I help out today?

At home
Take on one of the following: **28** Top a chore chart (p34); **44** Be a chef (p47); **50** Tell a LEGO® tale (p52).

Me!
Look after yourself: **58** Have sweet dreams (p58); **90** Celebrate the little things (p82); **94** And breeeeathe! (p85).

Animals
Discover how you can help: **9** Be animal aware (p17); **37** Bee friendly (p42); **95** Be kind to furry friends (p86).

At school
Give one of these a go: **3** Boost positivity (p13); **60** Start a club (p60); **82** Volunteer at school (p76).

In my community
Why not try these? **46** Hunt for rainbows (p49); **57** Befriend an elderly person (p58); **75** Start a "library of things" (p72).

The wider world
Start here: **51** Be awesome and recycle (p53); **35** Lights out (p40); **96** Take a shower challenge (p87).

What are you in the mood for?

Being active
Break a sweat:
4 Ready, steady, grow... (p14);
18 3, 2, 1... run! (p25);
47 Become a team player (p50).

Fancy a team challenge?

Yes
Want to build with friends? Try one of these: **32** Start a chain of creativity (p37); **36** Solve it! (p41); **63** Build together (p62).

No
Playing alone? Take on one of these fun solo activities: **19** Go on a bug hunt (p26); **45** Celebrate you! (p48); **73** Focus your mind (p71).

Discovering something new
Try one of these:
62 Celebrate heroes (p61);
85 Start a special book club (p79); **87** Explore the world (p80).

Getting super creative
Take on a challenge:
17 Be a food-waste hero (p24); **33** Say cheese! (p38); **54** Celebrate where you live (p55).

Being dramatic
Put on a showstopping performance:
23 Sing for joy (p30); **43** Make your school sparkle (p46).

What's the weather like?

Bad!
Stay inside and try a new activity: **15** Create a family game (p22); **21** Discover your history (p29); **80** Read all about it! (p75).

Getting organized
Take on a challenge to begin sorting:
10 Become a tidying whizz (p18);
20 Give toys a new home (p28);
42 Swap it! (p45).

Beautiful!
Head outside with one of these: **12** Be a litter champion (p20);
77 Get outdoors! (p73); **84** Meet new critters (p78).

Or why not try something totally random?

How about one of these?
7 Save your pennies (p16);
25 Go on a pet adventure (p32);
97 Look around you! (p87).

Offer a hug

If someone in your family has woken up in a sad or grumpy mood, show them you care about them by giving them a squeeze! It's quick, it's free, and scientists have found that a good hug helps to reduce bad feelings. Share a hug and you'll both feel the happy benefits.

1

Pick up a friendship

Get back in touch with a friend you no longer see. Perhaps you now go to different schools or your buddy has moved away. If you live far apart, why not write a letter? You could become pen pals. Have fun telling each other what has been happening in your lives.

2

Boost positivity

Bring sunshine to every day with a gratitude box for home or school. Have fun building your LEGO® box together. Then write on a piece of paper one or two things each day that you are thankful for, and post them in the box. Take it in turns to read them out loud to each other for a positive start or end to your day.

You could top it with tiles for a smooth finish

Put plates at the bottom and build up with interlocking bricks at the sides

Pop your folded up pieces of paper in the box

Build it

Your box could have a lid if you have LEGO hinge pieces, or you could leave it open.

Ready, steady, grow...

Look for volunteering groups in your area to see if you could help plant a tree at a local park or woods. Trees absorb pollution and help clean the air. Why not build a fun LEGO tree first for inspiration?

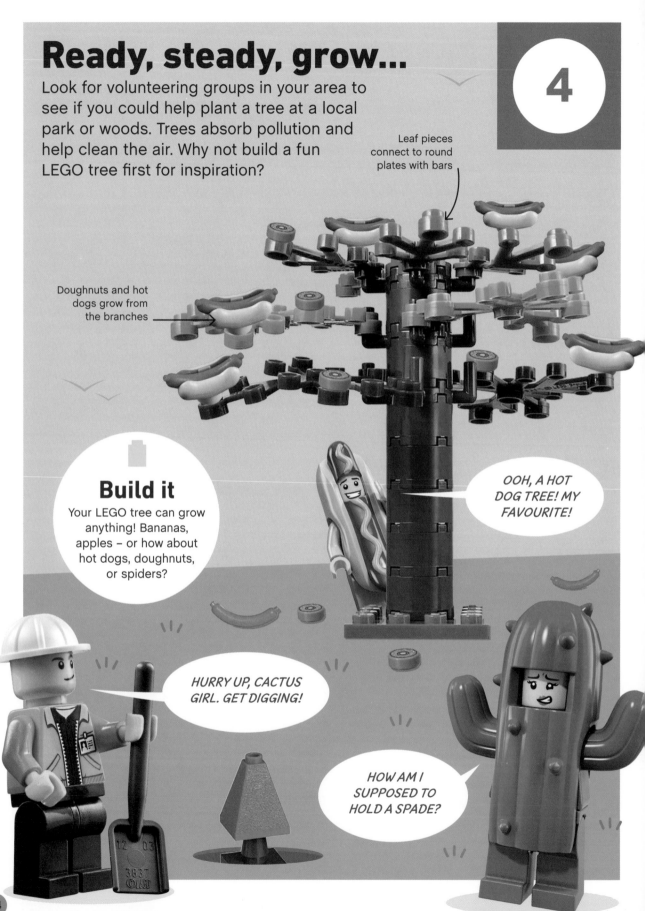

Leaf pieces connect to round plates with bars

Doughnuts and hot dogs grow from the branches

Build it
Your LEGO tree can grow anything! Bananas, apples – or how about hot dogs, doughnuts, or spiders?

OOH, A HOT DOG TREE! MY FAVOURITE!

HURRY UP, CACTUS GIRL. GET DIGGING!

HOW AM I SUPPOSED TO HOLD A SPADE?

5 Get moving!

Help cut down on pollution by cycling or walking when you can, instead of travelling by car. You might even spot some interesting wildlife on your way!

6 Give a thank-you card

Make somebody's day a little brighter. Build a LEGO card and decorate it to say thank you to a neighbour, bus driver, or teacher. Design a nice message to go inside.

Save your pennies

Build a LEGO piggy bank and learn to save money. Even better, why not build three? One for spending, one for saving, and one for sharing – buy someone a birthday gift or a treat.

7

OINK OINK!

Make sure the slot is big enough to put your money in

Build it

Your piggy bank can be any shape you like. It just needs to be hollow, with a slot to put money in.

Snout is made with a brick with two holes

Make someone laugh

Telling a joke is a laughing matter. Get creative and write your own jokes, or memorize a few favourites and cheer up your family members and friends. It will tickle your funny bones, too!

8

HE DIDN'T HAVE THE GUTS FOR IT!

WHY WOULDN'T THE SKELETON GO SKYDIVING?

Be animal aware

9

Find out about endangered animals from books or online. Why not build an animal with LEGO bricks and share what you have learned at a "show and tell" at school? The more we know about endangered animals, the more we can help them.

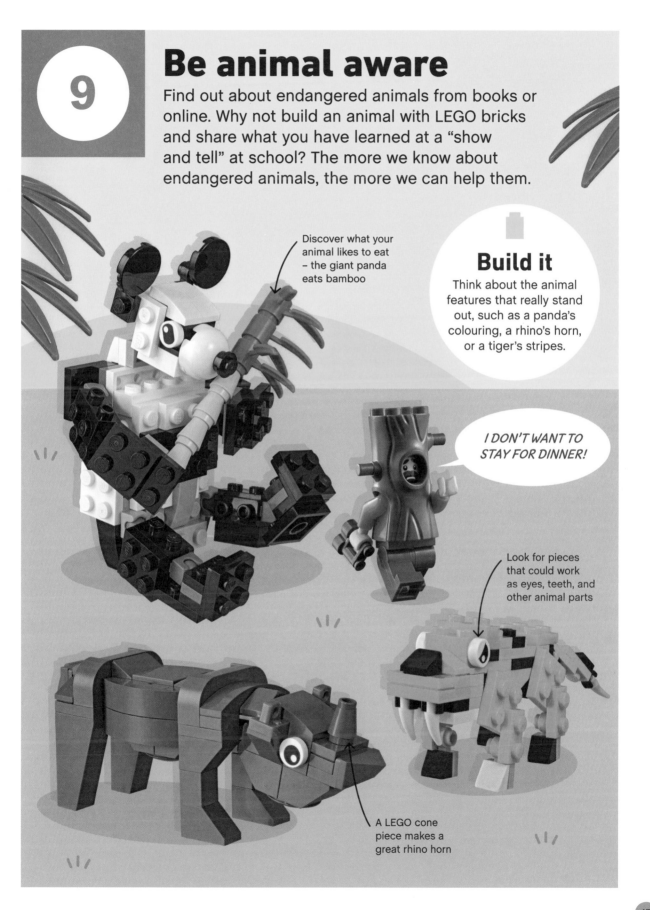

Discover what your animal likes to eat – the giant panda eats bamboo

Build it

Think about the animal features that really stand out, such as a panda's colouring, a rhino's horn, or a tiger's stripes.

I DON'T WANT TO STAY FOR DINNER!

Look for pieces that could work as eyes, teeth, and other animal parts

A LEGO cone piece makes a great rhino horn

Become a tidying whizz

"Tidy your room!" It's the chore that can be a bore, but there are ways to make it more fun! Put some music on, race against the clock, or be inspired by your LEGO bricks. Look around you for what you could declutter. Why not build a LEGO pen pot to keep your desk tidy? What else could you build for your room?

Build it

Start by thinking about what needs to fit in your desk tidy. Then think about colours or a fun theme.

Look to see if you have any special pieces that could work as a pot – like this barrel

A baseplate keeps everything stable

SHIVER ME TIMBERS! 'TIS THE TIDIEST ROOM I EVER DID SEE

A high tail supports bigger pens

A mythical sea monster can be any shape or colour you like!

Celebrate differences

Differences are great! The world would be a very dull place if everyone was the same. Get together with your friends and build each other as LEGO minifigures. Think about the many ways you are alike and different. We often find we love people precisely because they are not the same as us.

Minifigures could look like your friends or reflect their personalities or hobbies in some way

Be a litter champion

Help out in your community – and make it a prettier place to live. Neighbourhood organizations often hold seasonal clean-up days for tidying up parks and other public areas. Get outside with your family, put on some gloves, and start clearing.

12

Use recycling bins where appropriate

I'M GIVING LITTER THE BRUSH-OFF!

Share your skills

Are you a whizz at something? Playing an instrument, card tricks, or building with LEGO bricks? If so, don't keep your skill to yourself. Teach it to a friend! Why not teach them some LEGO building tips, such as how to build sideways?

13

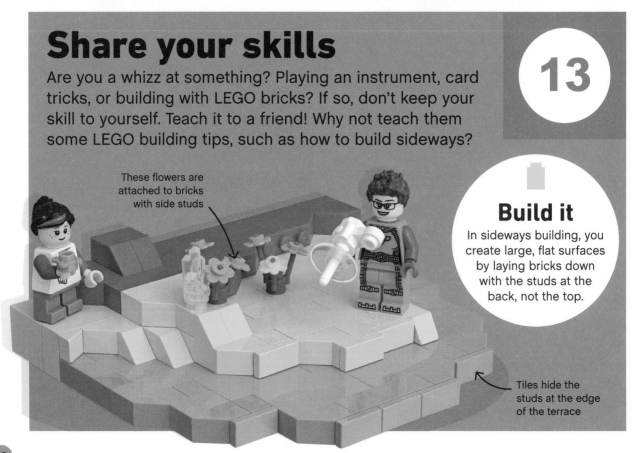

These flowers are attached to bricks with side studs

Build it
In sideways building, you create large, flat surfaces by laying bricks down with the studs at the back, not the top.

Tiles hide the studs at the edge of the terrace

Eat a rainbow

Fruit and vegetables are bursting with vitamins and minerals that keep us healthy and strong. We need at least five portions a day. Build a bumper crop of LEGO fruit and veg, and you might just find your appetite for the real thing beginning to grow!

14

Build it

Think about textures as well as shapes and colours, such as an avocado's knobbly skin.

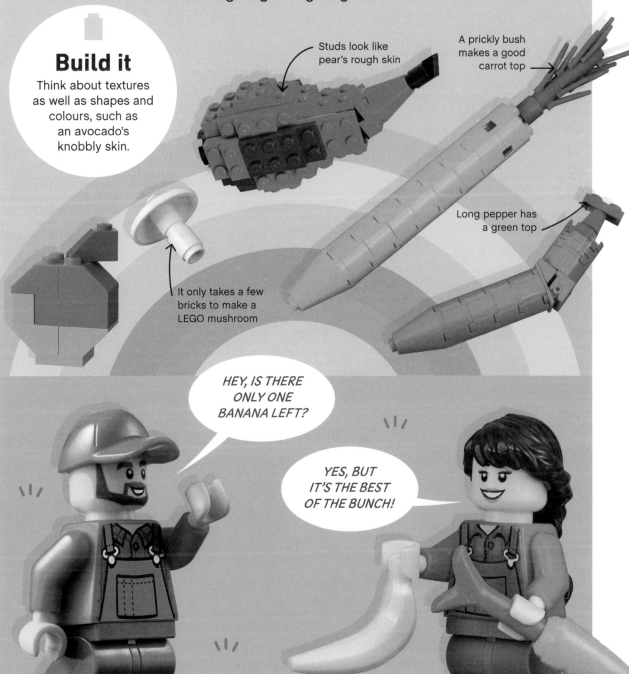

Studs look like pear's rough skin

A prickly bush makes a good carrot top

Long pepper has a green top

It only takes a few bricks to make a LEGO mushroom

HEY, IS THERE ONLY ONE BANANA LEFT?

YES, BUT IT'S THE BEST OF THE BUNCH!

Create a family game

Family time doesn't have to mean just watching TV together. Why not share some fun with your very own LEGO board game instead? Build a course, choose a finishing point, and draw up some rules. Pick a minifigure to represent each family member and get throwing that die!

15

Build it

Include a few special tiles. Landing on a lucky tile could win an extra throw; an unlucky one could send you back three places.

THIS LOOKS FUN. CAN I PLAY NEXT TIME?

Include some fun elements, like a palm tree on a treasure island build

ARRR... DAD'S BEATING ME TO THE TREASURE

Talk to the new kid

It can be daunting to join a new school or club. If you spot a newcomer, make sure to welcome them. Get chatting and help them to feel like one of the gang. You might have lots in common!

"Unlucky" tile printed with skull and crossbones

Find a die from another game

Be a food-waste hero

"Captain Cutlery here, with an important message. Nobody wastes food in this kitchen!" Build your very own food-waste super hero to remind your family not to throw food away. Think about all the ways you could waste less. Use up ripe fruit in cakes and pies, add spare vegetables to a soup, and turn leftovers into a new meal.

Build it

What tools and costume will your super hero have? Why not try adding a super hero cape?

FORKS AT THE READY! TUCK IN!

Sausage piece makes a smiling mouth

Hand is made of bricks with side studs, so the fork can attach

3, 2, 1... run!

Being active doesn't have to mean playing sports. Put music on and dance, head to the the playground, or play this fun LEGO building race with a friend. Exercise has so many amazing benefits. It gives us an energy boost, helps us to sleep better, and makes us feel happier. What are you waiting for?

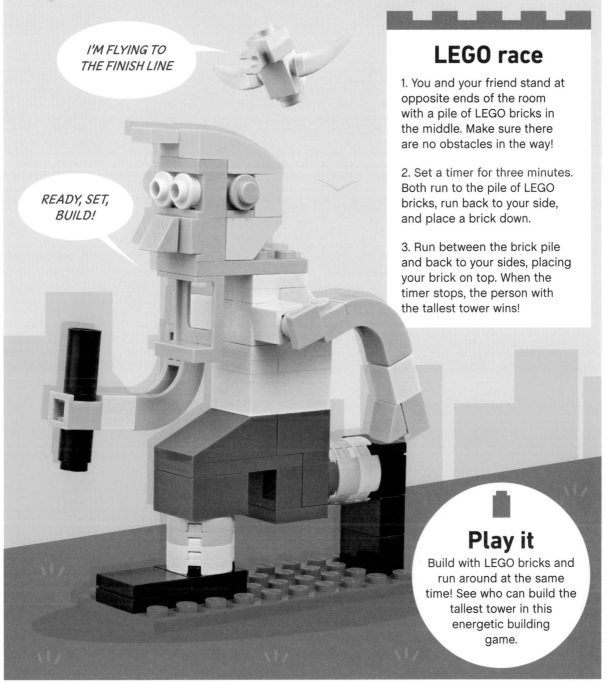

LEGO race

1. You and your friend stand at opposite ends of the room with a pile of LEGO bricks in the middle. Make sure there are no obstacles in the way!

2. Set a timer for three minutes. Both run to the pile of LEGO bricks, run back to your side, and place a brick down.

3. Run between the brick pile and back to your sides, placing your brick on top. When the timer stops, the person with the tallest tower wins!

Play it

Build with LEGO bricks and run around at the same time! See who can build the tallest tower in this energetic building game.

Go on a bug hunt

19

Be a minibeast detective and head out on an adventure to your local woodlands or park to learn about the important creatures that live there. Many bugs like to live in dark, damp places. Peek under logs or rocks, peer into cracks in bark and walls, and poke your nose into long grass. When home, build LEGO versions of the coolest creepy-crawlies you found.

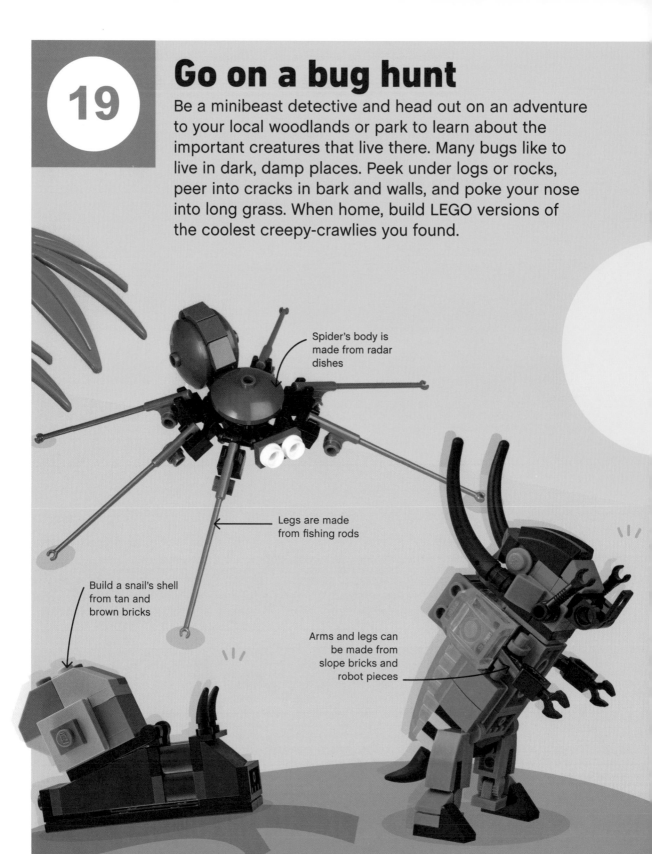

Spider's body is made from radar dishes

Legs are made from fishing rods

Build a snail's shell from tan and brown bricks

Arms and legs can be made from slope bricks and robot pieces

Remember Minibeasts are small and probably scared of you. Don't pick them up or move them from where you found them.

Green tail pieces make distinctive grasshopper legs

Long, transparent-green pieces are perfect for dragonfly wings

Build it

Look for unusual pieces that can work as antennae, legs, and shells. Be realistic with colour, or get creative with your own colourful creations.

Beetle's antennae are black plant pieces

NOBODY WARNED ME THEY WOULD BE THIS BIG!

Give toys a new home

Are there any toys you haven't played with in a long time? Pass on your old toys to younger friends or neighbours. Give the toys a clean and make sure that there aren't any missing pieces. It can be hard to part with old toys, but knowing your unused toys will be loved by somebody else will make you feel good.

THIS WAS MY FAVOURITE TOY WHEN I WAS A YOUNG ROBOT

YOU'LL LOVE PLAYING WITH MY OLD TOYS!

Discover your history

Talk to an older relative about your family history.
You're bound to learn a lot! Build a LEGO® family tree
to include your grandparents, parents, aunts and uncles,
cousins, brothers and sisters – and, of course, you!

AHOY THERE, LITTLE'UNS!

Grandparents are on the top layer

Branches are long plates sandwiched between bricks in the trunk

Include pets, too!

Build it

Begin with yourself
and siblings or cousins
at the bottom, and put
your oldest relatives
at the top.

Minifigures could look like
your family members, or
reflect their personalities,
jobs, or hobbies

Love yourself

Remember – you are special! Build a LEGO heart to show yourself some love. Place it on your shelf as a reminder when you need it that you are good enough just the way you are. Your LEGO heart could be one colour or a mixture of colours.

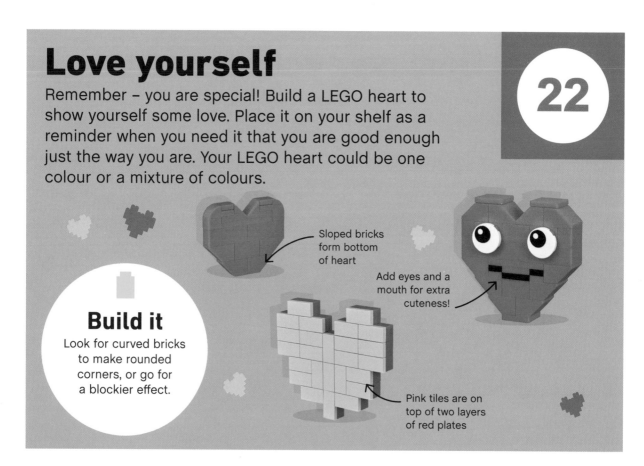

Sloped bricks form bottom of heart

Add eyes and a mouth for extra cuteness!

Build it
Look for curved bricks to make rounded corners, or go for a blockier effect.

Pink tiles are on top of two layers of red plates

Sing for joy

La la la la la la la! There are so many reasons why singing makes us happy. It releases feel-good chemicals in the brain and it makes us feel energized. Why not sing with your friends or neighbours, or join a group? It's fun to sing together. Or you could get creative and make up your own songs!

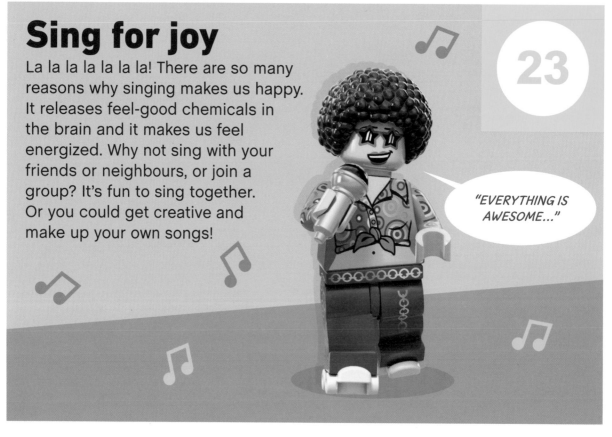

"EVERYTHING IS AWESOME..."

24 Host an awards night

"Ladies and gentlemen, your host tonight is... me!" Celebrate all the amazing things that your friends or family do by putting on an awards ceremony. Just hearing why you think they are awesome will make their day. Will you give an award to the best hugger, the friend who always makes you laugh, or the bravest spider remover? Build LEGO trophies to make your ceremony extra special.

Build it

Build two sturdy arms for holding the trophy triumphantly in the air.

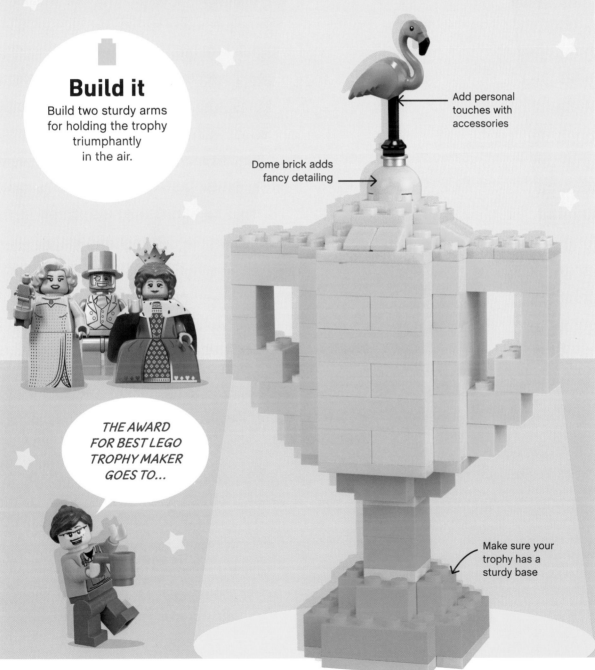

Add personal touches with accessories

Dome brick adds fancy detailing

THE AWARD FOR BEST LEGO TROPHY MAKER GOES TO...

Make sure your trophy has a sturdy base

Go on a pet adventure

Build a LEGO pet. It could be a cat, a duck, an elephant – or even an alien! Choose a name and take turns with friends, classmates, or family members to "look after" your pet and take it on adventures. Where will you go? For a walk, to the park, on a picnic...? After a few days, tell your friends or family all about your exciting experiences.

Build it
You could look for unusual pieces in your LEGO collection and let that guide you with what to build.

QUACK!

Alien's legs connect to a ring with bar segments

Duck's feet and beak are orange slope bricks

Make your pet any colour you like!

Tail pieces look great as tusks

DON'T FORGET TO TAKE PHOTOS!

Share it!

Sharing is caring! Do something nice for a friend or your brother or sister and share your snack or a toy. You'll probably find that they will return the kind deed and share something with you!

Be kind online

Treat others online the same as you would if you were face to face. Positive messages, comments, and emojis will give your friends a real boost. Keep to your agreed rules for online safety and always tell a grown-up if you are concerned about anything you see.

Top a chore chart

Chores! Ugh! They may not be fun, but they need to be done! It's not fair if the grown-ups do all the chores, so talk to them about which daily tasks you could take on to help out at home. The fun bit? Build a cute LEGO chore chart to keep track of your good deeds.

28

Build it

Build a little scene with space to stack a brick each time you finish a task.

This stack shows how many times you have taken the dog for a walk

THESE DISHES ARE SPOTLESS!

You have washed the dishes three times!

Bring the birthday joy

A grown-up's birthday often goes by unnoticed. Make a relative or neighbour's birthday extra special by surprising them with a LEGO birthday cake. Don't forget the candle!

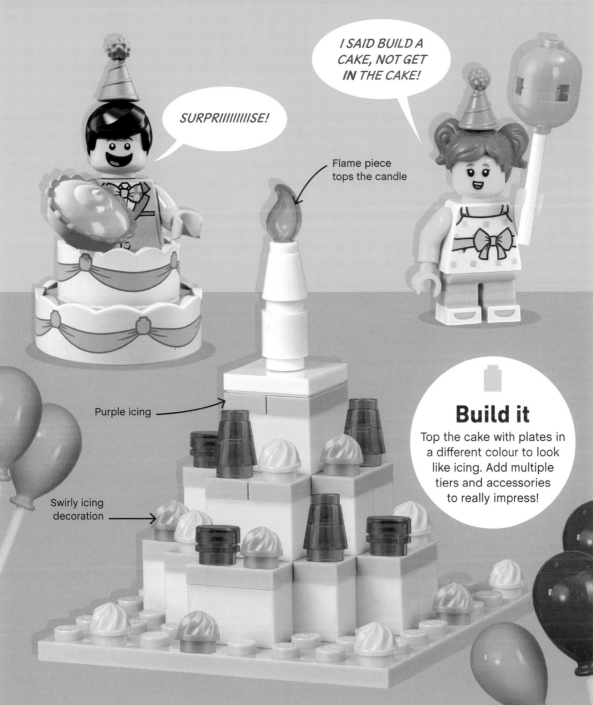

I SAID BUILD A CAKE, NOT GET IN THE CAKE!

SURPRIIIIIIIIISE!

Flame piece tops the candle

Purple icing

Swirly icing decoration

Build it

Top the cake with plates in a different colour to look like icing. Add multiple tiers and accessories to really impress!

Help a classmate

Do you find maths a doddle or are you a writing whizz? If you're good at something at school, why not offer to help a friend who isn't so confident? Don't actually do their work for them, but share your ideas or talk through how you solved a problem.

I'M REALLY STRUGGLING TO WRITE THIS

I THINK YOU NEED A SMALLER PENCIL!

Offer your seat

Show you care by giving up your chair! Look around you when on a bus or train or in a waiting area to see if somebody might need it. If there is somebody elderly, frail, pregnant, or who has a baby or very small children, ask them if they would like your seat.

WOULD YOU LIKE TO SIT DOWN?

YES PLEASE, DEAR!

32

Start a chain of creativity

Spread creativity among your friends. The best thing about this fun timed game is that anything goes! What fun creations can you build together? When you've finished, talk about what your creations could be. The sillier the better!

Play it

All you need to start a chain of creativity is a large pile of LEGO bricks, your friends, and a timer.

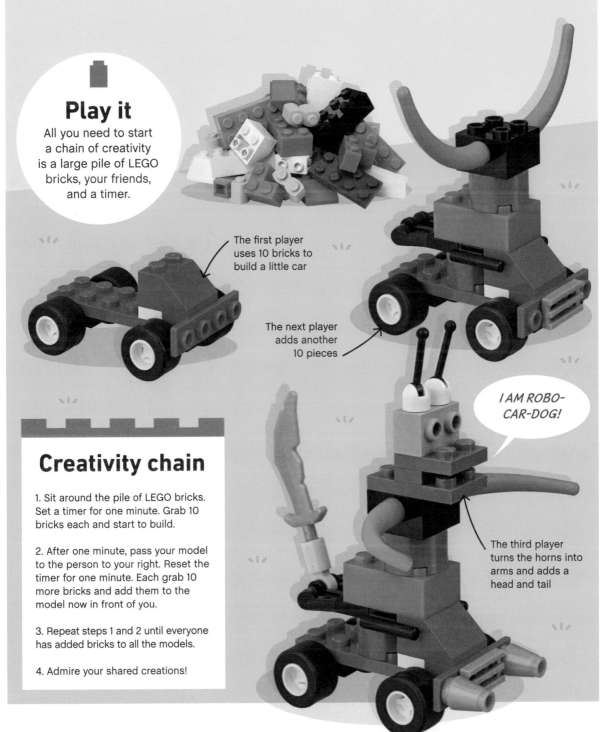

The first player uses 10 bricks to build a little car

The next player adds another 10 pieces

I AM ROBO-CAR-DOG!

The third player turns the horns into arms and adds a head and tail

Creativity chain

1. Sit around the pile of LEGO bricks. Set a timer for one minute. Grab 10 bricks each and start to build.

2. After one minute, pass your model to the person to your right. Reset the timer for one minute. Each grab 10 more bricks and add them to the model now in front of you.

3. Repeat steps 1 and 2 until everyone has added bricks to all the models.

4. Admire your shared creations!

Say cheese!

Looking at a photo of your family or friends can make you feel happy inside! Take a new photo or find an old favourite. Ask a grown-up to help you print the photo, and then build a cool LEGO photo frame to put by your bed.

Build it

Measure your photo first so you know how big to build the photo frame.

CHEEEESEE!

Build two identical rectangles and add a middle layer of one-stud-wide plates to hold the rectangles together

Decorate your frame any way you like!

Leave a gap on one side of the frame with no middle layer so there is space for the photo to slide in

Be the news

Is there something you feel passionate about? Not everyone will share your passion, but they might like to learn more. You could offer to write a story for your school newsletter or present the topic to your class.

Lights out

Start a family "lights out challenge" to help everyone to remember to switch off lights when they leave a room. Every time you remember to turn off the lights, you gain one minute of your favourite activity. But every time you forget, you lose a minute!

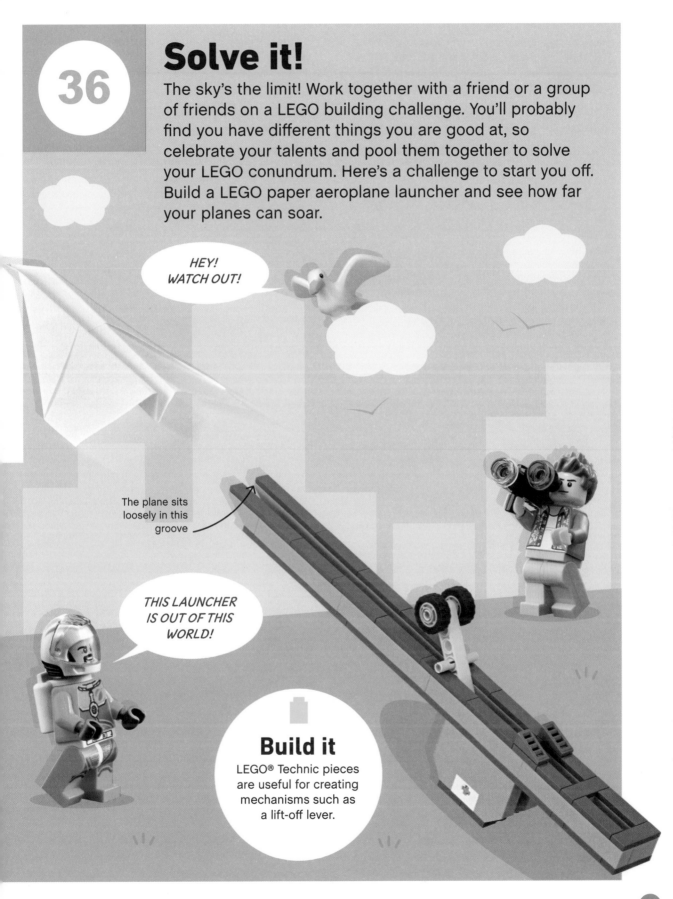

Solve it!

36

The sky's the limit! Work together with a friend or a group of friends on a LEGO building challenge. You'll probably find you have different things you are good at, so celebrate your talents and pool them together to solve your LEGO conundrum. Here's a challenge to start you off. Build a LEGO paper aeroplane launcher and see how far your planes can soar.

HEY! WATCH OUT!

The plane sits loosely in this groove

THIS LAUNCHER IS OUT OF THIS WORLD!

Build it

LEGO® Technic pieces are useful for creating mechanisms such as a lift-off lever.

Bee friendly

Bzzzz! Bees need our help! These important insects help to pollinate plants, but their numbers are dropping. Encourage bees to your garden by growing flowers such as sunflowers, nasturtiums, lavender, and honeysuckle. Build some LEGO flowers and bees to spread the message at a "show and tell" at school.

Transparent bricks make fluttering wings

Bee's legs are antenna pieces

Slope bricks for leaves

WELCOME, BEES!

A collection of small green bricks stack to create a stem

Build it

Look for colourful pieces that could work as flower petals and add a base to ensure your plant can balance.

38 Welcome everyone

Organize a LEGO games afternoon – and don't just invite your closest friends. Ask someone you haven't invited before. It is kind to include others and it's a great opportunity to foster new friendships. Play a fun LEGO game like this creative 'bots challenge!

'Bots challenge

1. Sit with your friends around a big pile of LEGO pieces. Set a timer for 10 minutes, and start building.

2. See who can build the quirkiest robots before the time runs out!

3. Play again with another theme – why not try building cars, farmyard animals, or scary monsters?

Play it

Build any robot you want in this timed building challenge. The quirkier the better!

39 Have your say

If you get a chance to speak up about an issue at school, make sure your voice is heard. It could be about anything from special events to snack-time ideas. Join in discussions at class circle times, write ideas in a suggestions box, and vote in school elections.

WHAT ABOUT A FANCY DRESS DAY?

I THINK THERE SHOULD BE MORE BANANAS!

Step into their shoes

It's always good to think about other people's feelings. If your friend does not seem their usual self, ask yourself some questions: How do you think they are feeling? Why might they be feeling that way? What could you do to help? Building a LEGO® emoji might just bring a smile to your friend's face!

Build it

Use different coloured plates to create facial expressions. You could also build another expression on the other side!

YOUR SMILE IS EVEN BIGGER THAN MINE!

Doubling up the plates makes an even bigger smile!

A small plate gives a wink

These black plates create a smile

Be brave

41

Stepping out of your comfort zone can be nerve-racking, but it can be exciting too! Is there something you feel worried about trying? Chances are you'll feel proud if you give it a go. What will you do? Jump off the diving board? Join a new club? Sleep over at a friend's house?

Swap it!

42

Grown out of your clothes? Need an outfit for a fancy dress event? Organize a clothes swap! Get grown-ups involved and have fun finding "new" clothes for free! Set the date before a change of season and invite friends and neighbours!

Make your school sparkle

Contribute to your school by helping to organize a fun event. What about a class talent show where students can showcase their skills, such as singing, dancing, sports, acting, magic, or comedy? Talk to your teacher for advice on how to set it up – and build yourself a LEGO microphone to really look the part!

Build it
A mix of slope and curved bricks will give your microphone a rounded look.

All the bricks are upside down!

THIS SONG ROCKS!

Long antenna piece →

Be a chef

Pop your chef's hat on and lend a hand at mealtimes. There are lots of ways you can get involved – stirring, whisking, measuring ingredients, cracking eggs, or crumbling cheese. Don't forget to set the table too! Get inspired and plan your meals with LEGO bricks.

Build it

Whip up your favourite foods with LEGO bricks. Adding eyes will ensure they are far too cute to eat!

BON APPETIT!

Pale yellow bricks for corn cob

Lemony icing and cake layers form a delicious lemon slice

Cheese slice peeks out of the sandwich

Celebrate you!

Express yourself by building a LEGO model or picking a minifigure to show the world who you really are. Is there a hobby, animal, or something else that represents your likes or personality in an awesome way?

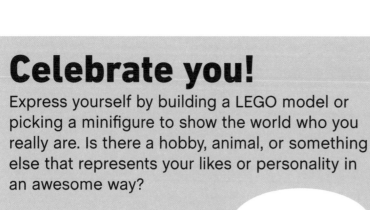

Hunt for rainbows

Add a splash of colour to your neighbourhood by building a LEGO rainbow and placing it by a window to bring a smile to people walking by. See if other children in the neighbourhood would like to get involved, and go on a rainbow hunt to see how many you can spot!

Stack bricks in a staircase shape

I LOVE RAINBOWS!

White bricks for clouds

Baseplate is the colour of the sky

Build it
You could build a 3-D model or a flat design on a baseplate, which you can prop up in your window.

Adding a grin to your model is sure to make passers-by smile

Become a team player

Join a team and you'll learn patience, trust, and teamwork – all while making friends and having fun along the way. Don't feel you need to do what your friends do. Follow your interests – you could join a sports team, quiz team, or chess team. You might even pick up a trophy or two!

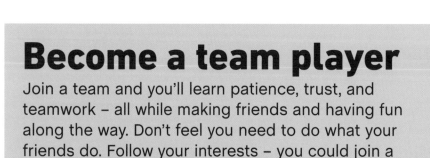

GOOOAALLL!

The goalie has some gloves made from tiles

This top scorer has the minifigure-head ball

AWESOME FOOTWORK!

Attach head to body with a round stud

Build it
Build team spirit by creating your team with LEGO bricks, making each model look like a real-life member.

Borrow kindly

48

Be a brilliant borrower! If a friend lends you something, treat it with care. Don't let it get dirty or damaged, and whatever you do, don't lose it. Give it back when you say you will, too. That way, your friend will know they can trust you to borrow other things in future.

THANKS! I HAD FUN WITH THIS

YOU'RE WELCOME!

Turn off the tap

49

Did you know that if you brush your teeth for two minutes and leave the tap running, you'll be wasting up to 10 litres (2.5 gallons) of water? Save precious water and turn off that tap! Build a LEGO toothbrush and place it next to the tap to help remind you!

Build it

Use long plates and slope bricks for your toothbrush, and add white bricks for the bristles.

WHOOPS! I CAN'T CLEAN MY TEETH WITH THIS BRUSH!

Tell a LEGO® tale

"Once upon a time there was a LEGO fan who built a story..." Entertain your younger brothers, sisters, or friends by telling them a story using your LEGO bricks. You could tell a LEGO version of a well-known tale, such as the Three Billy Goats Gruff, or invent a story of your own filled with monsters, princesses, dragons – or whatever your imagination dreams up!

I'M GOING TO RESCUE A PRINCESS FROM A TOWER...

THANKS! BUT I'M QUITE HAPPY UP HERE!

Three scenes tell the story of the prince, princess, and dragon

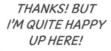

Build it
Keep your scenes small and simple, focusing on a few key moments in the story.

SEE! THERE'S A FIRE-BREATHING DRAGON DOWN HERE!

Move the minifigure characters across the different scenes

Be awesome and recycle

Did you know that more than half of what goes into the average bin could be recycled? Challenge your family to reduce the amount of rubbish you produce each day by throwing your paper, glass, tins, and single-use plastic into recycling bins.

Make someone feel great

Compliments cost nothing, so sprinkle them freely. Admire a shop assistant's necklace or your teacher's new shoes. Tell a friend she's the best dancer in the class. It will make them feel great – and seeing their happy faces will make you feel good, too.

WOW... YOUR NEW HAIRCUT LOOKS AMAZING!

REALLY? AW, THANKS!

Unplug it!

Save energy by unplugging! When something is plugged in – whether it is switched on or off – it still uses electricity. Make it a habit to unplug your phone charger, computer, television, and other small devices as much as possible. Always leave the fridge and freezer plugged in, though!

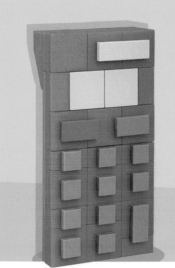

PHEW... IT'S GOING TO TAKE ALL MY ENERGY TO DISCONNECT THIS

Celebrate where you live

Show some love for your local area by making a LEGO logo depicting all that's good about it. Is there a famous building? A distinctive bridge? Some awesome trees? Is it by a beach or a lake? Ask your friends what their favourite things about your neighbourhood are, too, so you come up with a design that will make everyone proud.

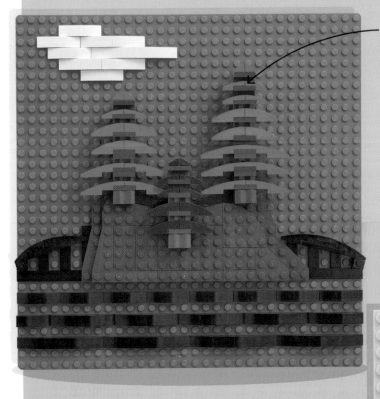

Build up details in layers to give a 3-D look

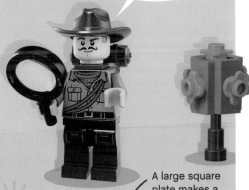

THIS PLACE LOOKS TREE-MENDOUS!

A large square plate makes a good base

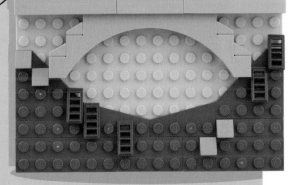

Clouds are overlapping round bricks

Build it

It's a good idea to sketch out your idea first so you can work out colours and proportions.

Go bird-watching

Birds don't just look pretty, they help to control pests, pollinate plants, and spread seeds, too. We should take care to preserve the habitats of birds, especially rare ones. What birds can you spot on a woodland walk, in a city park, or by a lake? Use books or look online to identify them. Then build the beautiful birds you have seen out of LEGO bricks.

This woodpecker's neck is hinged, so it can really peck

Try to match the bird's colours – blue bricks are perfect for this kingfisher

If you don't have a special eye piece, a small, round brick would work too

Build it

Tooth plates are really useful for building birds – they make great beaks, feet, and feather tips.

*IT'S **SO** BUSY HERE TODAY!*

Take care! Birds scare easily, so keep your distance when bird-watching and don't make any loud noises.

Look on the bright side

A bad day at school or cross words with a friend can sometimes send your mood into a downward spiral. Don't let that happen! Staying positive will help you to keep these little setbacks in proportion. Focus on nice things instead. Plan a day out, read a book, or play with your LEGO bricks. You'll be looking on the bright side again in no time!

Slope bricks work as tails, feathers, and beaks

You could include a tree for your bird to perch on

Befriend an elderly person

Elderly people might feel lonely, especially if they don't get out much. Why not befriend some elderly neighbours? You could chat to your new friends over the fence about what it was like to be your age years ago, and tell them about what it is like to be a child now.

THIS IS MY FAVOURITE LEGO MODEL

Have sweet dreams

You've heard of counting sheep? Try counting LEGO minifigures as you fall asleep instead! It is important to get enough sleep – our bodies need it to repair and grow. If we don't get enough, we find it difficult to concentrate. Before bedtime, unwind by building some funny, silly LEGO characters to star in your dreams at night.

Borrow a minifigure hat for your funny character

Build it

Keep your pre-bedtime building simple. You don't want to stay up late trying to finish your builds!

59

Be fair!

Winning a game feels great if you've played fairly. Create a LEGO game with your friends. Will it be a board game that relies on lucky throws of a die? Or will it be a game of pure strategy, like draughts? Of course, there is one rule your games should always have: absolutely no cheating!

YOU GO FIRST... I WENT FIRST LAST TIME

THAT'S VERY FAIR OF YOU

Build it

Use plates in alternating colours to build a draughtboard, making sure there are eight or twelve squares at each edge.

Each player's draughts are a different colour so they don't get mixed up during the game

Start a club

A shared hobby is ten times the fun. How about starting an after-school club, such as a LEGO® club, with some classmates? You could play games, hold competitions, and join in epic group builds. Talk to your teacher for advice on how to get it started.

HERE'S YOUR BAND OF BRICKSTERS MEMBERSHIP CARD!

Surprise a pal

Don't wait for a special occasion to give a gift. Make a friend smile with a present inside a pretty LEGO gift box. What you put inside – a sweet, a bracelet, or that LEGO minifigure your friend has had their eye on – is up to you.

61

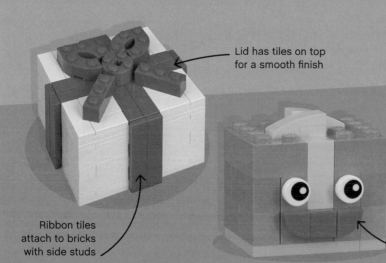

Lid has tiles on top for a smooth finish

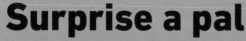

Build it

Begin with a simple box with plates at the bottom and bricks stacked at the sides. Then add a lid and decorations.

Ribbon tiles attach to bricks with side studs

Add facial features for a beaming box

Celebrate heroes

62

You don't have to wear a cape to be a hero! Heroes are all around us. Take a look through newspapers for local people who have been recognized for bravery, community service, or selfless acts. Look online or in books for people in history who have done something brave. Don't forget your family photos, too. Why not do a "show and tell" about someone who has made the world a better place?

I WANT TO BE JUST LIKE YOU WHEN I GROW UP!

Build together

Sharing ideas can expand your horizons – and your LEGO builds too! Get together with friends, choose a theme for a build, and start firing off ideas and suggestions on how to go about it. Make everyone responsible for a different part, such as different floors of a tall building. Put the model together and notice how similar – or different – the parts look.

Build it
The building sections can be created separately and then assembled into the final build at the end. This is called modular building.

Add as many storeys as there are builders

The team decided it was best to have a library at the top

There is a tiny restaurant on this floor

The ground floor has a flower shop

Host a book swap

Why not host a book swap party for your bookworm buddies? It's a great way of discovering new authors or trying books you'd never have picked up in a bookshop or at school. Just don't fight over the LEGO books!

Stand up for what's right

We all know we mustn't tolerate unkind behaviour, but it takes courage to stand up to it. It can help to think about what to say beforehand. Rehearse with your minifigures what you might say or do in certain situations. If you are worried about any unkind behaviour, always talk to a grown-up for advice.

66 Thank your teacher

Do you have a favourite teacher? Someone kind, funny, and inspiring, who makes learning fun? Show your appreciation with a small handmade gift or card. You could even revive an old tradition of bringing them an apple, but with a twist – make it with LEGO bricks!

Build it

Start with a circular base and then build upwards. Step the bricks outwards and then in to form a round shape.

Add a stem and leaf for a freshly picked look

Bricks form the main shape, and small plates help to make it look rounded

WOW! I'M TOUCHED TO THE CORE!

IT'S FOR YOU, SIR

Be a good neighbour

Help to build a friendly community around you by making a difference to a neighbour's day. Offer to take out an elderly person's rubbish bins, sweep leaves off someone's driveway, and take time to greet newcomers.

67

Say no to rubbish

Picnics are perfect – and you can make yours a rubbish-free lunch! Bring a drink in a reusable bottle, food in a lunchbox, and cutlery from home.

68

Start a worm farm

69

Worms are amazing little environmentalists. They eat microbes from food scraps, turning them into compost. It's easy to start a worm farm in a compost bin or bucket. Read up about it online first so you know how to keep your worms happy and healthy. You'll soon be the proud owner of a colony of wrigglers – and you may notice other visitors, too!

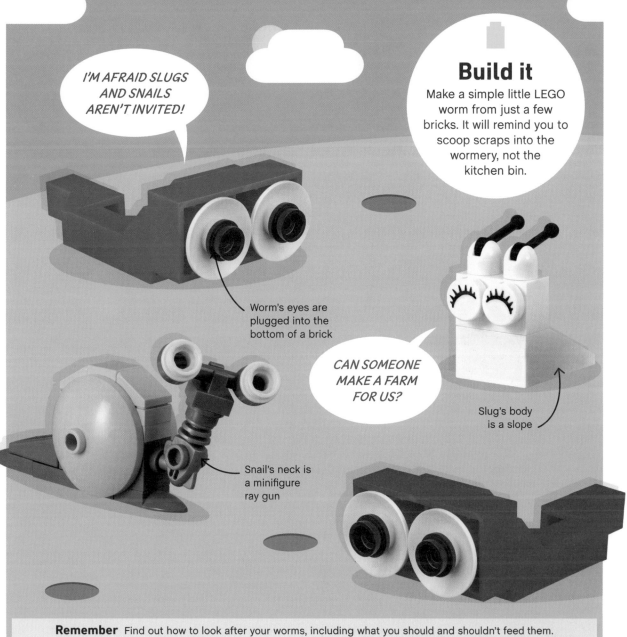

I'M AFRAID SLUGS AND SNAILS AREN'T INVITED!

Build it

Make a simple little LEGO worm from just a few bricks. It will remind you to scoop scraps into the wormery, not the kitchen bin.

Worm's eyes are plugged into the bottom of a brick

CAN SOMEONE MAKE A FARM FOR US?

Slug's body is a slope

Snail's neck is a minifigure ray gun

Remember Find out how to look after your worms, including what you should and shouldn't feed them.

Be their biggest fan

Sometimes we can feel jealous when a friend does something we wish we could do, such as acing a test or scoring a goal. Push those jealous feelings aside, congratulate your friend, and you will feel much better. Build a LEGO number "1" to show your pal just how fabulous you think they are.

70

Build it

Your brick-built number could be one colour or a mixture of colours. You could decorate it with accessories, too!

LEGO numbers also make cool decorations for birthdays or important dates

YOU'RE **ONE** OF A KIND!

1

Wish them well

If someone you love is sick or in pain, do something nice for them to show them you care. Deliver a treat, draw them a picture, create a little care package, or surprise them with a glorious bunch of LEGO flowers.

LEGO blooms last a lot longer than real flowers! →

← Look for unusual pieces in your collection

Stems attach to plate to stay upright →

THANKS A BUNCH!

Build it

Stack round green bricks for the stems. Colourful curved slopes work well for petals.

Respect the rules

It might feel like you're always having to follow rules!
Waiting for a green man when crossing the road, wearing
a bike helmet, not running in the school corridors – the
list is long, but all the rules are there to keep us safe
and well. Respect the rules at school, at home, and in
the wider world, and encourage others to do the same.
Luckily, there are no rules when building with LEGO bricks!

IS THIS LIGHT EVER GOING TO TURN GREEN?

73

Focus your mind

If you feel like you have too many thoughts racing round your head, try to pay attention to just one sense at a time. This could be what you see, hear, smell, taste, or feel. Practise with this fun minifigure guessing game.

Who's in the bag?

1. Place a few minifigures inside a fabric bag or sock.
2. Set a timer for one minute, close your eyes, and feel one minifigure through the bag. Really focus your attention on what you can feel.
3. After one minute, take the minifigure out. Did you guess it correctly? Repeat until you've guessed them all – just with your sense of touch!

Play it

Can you identify minifigures just by how they feel? Close your eyes and focus your mind.

74

Be kind, tidy!

Always offer to tidy up before leaving a friend's house. Make this part of playtime – see who can pick up the most number of toys in three minutes, or put some music on and have a dance party while you tidy!

OH, I FORGOT THAT LARGE BLUE BRICK

HEY, I'M NOT A BRICK!

Start a "library of things"

As a family, set up a community "library of things" to share objects with friends and neighbours. Create a list of things that you don't use often, such as tools, costumes, and board games, which everyone else can add to. Simply send an email when you'd like to borrow something.

Be a kindness detective

If you are feeling sad about something, it can sometimes be hard to pick yourself up. Put on your (invisible) detective hat and look around you to see all the little acts of kindness that people are doing for each other every single day. You probably won't have to look far.

Get outdoors!

77

Being outside isn't just fun, it's good for us too! We get a dose of vitamin D, which is important for healthy bones. Try to do something outdoors every day, such as going on a walk, heading to the park, playing sports, or having a picnic. And if the weather's really bad, have fun putting together a LEGO model of your favourite outdoor activity instead!

Build it

Add little details to your outdoors scene, such as sports equipment, food, and animals.

Add flowers or build a tree for shade

EATING PIE OUTSIDE IS EVEN BETTER THAN EATING PIE INSIDE!

Build a juice carton with a small brick and slope brick on top

Two long plates make up this bench

Treat someone

Show someone you care by surprising them with their favourite sweet treat! A baked goody is sure to brighten their day – whether it's a homemade cupcake, a brownie from their favourite bakery, or even a LEGO cookie! See what delicious-looking creations you can build with your LEGO bricks.

Build it

You only need a handful of bricks to build a simple biscuit or cake. Add layers or even icing for fancier bakes.

Use a white round plate for a layer of cream

Don't forget icing and a cherry for your bun!

Build a rectangle shape for traybakes like brownies

LEGO Battenberg cake has pink and yellow bricks inside

AW! THANK YOU, DEAR. THAT'S SO SWEET!

Grow vegetables

79

If you have access to an outdoor space, why not plant a vegetable patch? By growing your own vegetables or herbs you won't have to visit the shops as much, and you'll get lots of fresh air outside.

Build it

Use your LEGO bricks to plan what to grow. Build some LEGO veggies and arrange them together in a LEGO garden.

This vegetable patch might need a scarecrow to keep birds away!

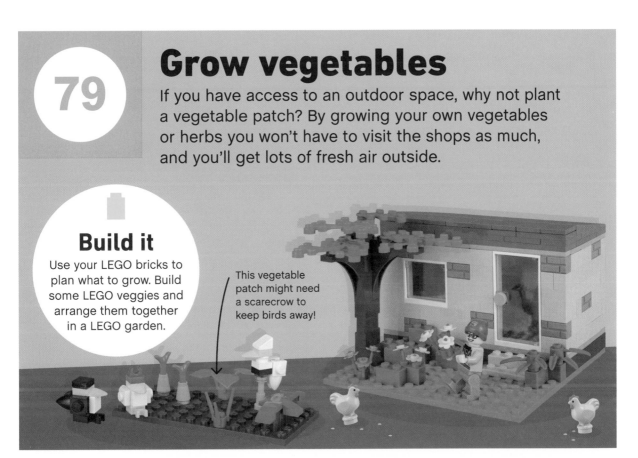

Read all about it!

80

Start a "good news" newspaper full of positive stories. If you hear about someone doing something kind or a story with a happy ending, write about it in your paper. Once you have collected enough stories, spread the cheer by handing out copies to your family and friends.

THE NEIGHBOURS' LOST CAT HAS BEEN FOUND SAFE AND SOUND!

Listen to others

Take part in a friendly discussion about a topic that is important to you. Speak up about what you believe in, but remember that it is important to listen to other people's points of view as well. Stay positive and respectful, and see what you can learn from others.

Volunteer at school

Be a superstar at school by finding ways to help out your busy teachers. Get into the habit of returning books after you use them, putting away sports equipment at the end of a sports lesson, and picking up litter when you see it. Helping out with little tasks can make a huge difference.

Give a thoughtful gift

83

Everyone likes to receive gifts, and gifts with a nice thought behind them are extra special. Give someone a gift that you think they'll really appreciate. For example, if your brother or sister struggles to spot their schoolbag, a brightly coloured bag charm will make it easier. If your friend loves watching videos on their phone, a phone stand will let them watch hands-free.

Build it

Use your friend's or family member's favourite colours to make their gift extra special.

Add your own design to a LEGO® bag charm piece

OOH, THIS PROGRAMME IS MY FAVOURITE!

Leave a gap for a phone to fit in

Meet new critters

Wildlife is everywhere! Take a trip to a beach, lake, river, or pond to learn about the different creatures that live there. When home, read about them in books or online to find out more. What kind of food do they eat, where do they sleep, and how do they look after their young? Now build them with your LEGO bricks!

Build it

Once you've built your critter, why not try building a little LEGO habitat, too?

Bulrushes are made from cones and bars

Stack blue bricks sideways for a duck pond

Frogs like to eat flies – this one is made from two tiny bricks

Beaver's webbed feet are LEGO flippers

Start a special book club

85

Love reading? Set up a book club – with a twist! Invite your friends or family to join, then take turns choosing a book that is about someone from a different background. The character could be from a different country or have a different type of family, for example. Give everyone a set amount of time to read it, then meet up to discuss.

Buy local

86

Have fun discovering what's on your doorstep and visit small shops. Get to know your local shop owners and cut down on pollution, too – especially if you walk! Encourage your family to buy local by shopping at a farmer's market or bakery, buying presents at a craft fair or boutique, and eating in family-owned restaurants and cafés.

Explore the world

There's a whole world out there! Be a global citizen by being curious about other places and cultures. Challenge yourself to go online or visit a library to learn about as many different countries as you can. Learn about what life might be like for a child your age who lives there, and use your bricks to build something from the countries you learn about.

Japan has beautiful castles that were built by noblemen many years ago →

Build it

You could build animals, buildings, food, transportation, people... anything! Use pictures for reference.

← Red plates for blossom

Tiny transparent bricks make perfect windows for micro skyscrapers

Give a helping hand

88

Look out for opportunities to help people throughout the day. It could be holding a door open, letting someone with just a few items go in front of you at a shop till, or helping a teacher to carry something. Don't be afraid to ask other people for help when you need it, too!

Caption from image: I'LL HOLD YOUR ICE LOLLY FOR YOU!

I CAN'T HOLD ANYTHING IN THIS COSTUME!

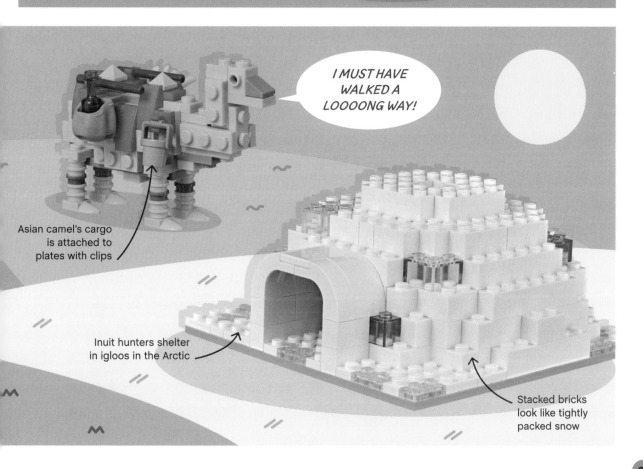

I MUST HAVE WALKED A LOOOONG WAY!

Asian camel's cargo is attached to plates with clips

Inuit hunters shelter in igloos in the Arctic

Stacked bricks look like tightly packed snow

89

Save paper

When you're busy practising your painting skills or writing up your plans to rebuild the world, remember to double up to save paper. Once you've used one side of a piece of paper, simply flip it over. You'll halve the amount of paper you get through!

DON'T FORGET TO USE BOTH SIDES OF THE PAPER!

90

Celebrate the little things

Build yourself a LEGO medal for something you are proud of, however small. Perhaps you spoke up in class, finished a school project, or helped a friend with a problem. Hang the medal to remind yourself when you need it that you are awesome.

Build it

Add a number figure to your medals to mark different achievements – add two layers of small round plates.

Thread ribbon through this hole to hang the medal in your room

Make more than one to remind you of different things you are proud of

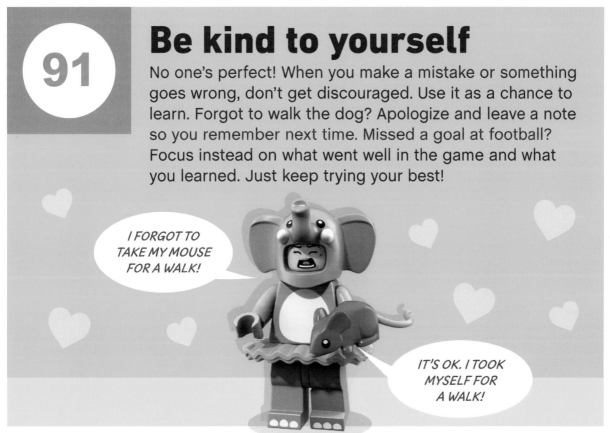

Be kind to yourself

91

No one's perfect! When you make a mistake or something goes wrong, don't get discouraged. Use it as a chance to learn. Forgot to walk the dog? Apologize and leave a note so you remember next time. Missed a goal at football? Focus instead on what went well in the game and what you learned. Just keep trying your best!

Do something you love every day

Make time to do something that makes you happy every single day – even if it's just for five minutes. Whether it's building with your LEGO bricks, drawing a picture, or playing an instrument, making time for something you love is an important way to look after yourself. Challenge yourself to build a LEGO model in five minutes as a fun way to start or end your day.

Tools work as bug antennae and legs

Create a little scene with just a handful of bricks

Transparent pieces for robot's eyes

Build it

Be inspired by a single piece. A cone could be a beak, or a radar dish could be a penguin's tummy.

Printed radar dish looks like an owl's feathery tummy

93 Plant a butterfly paradise

Grow plants like lavender and marjoram to encourage butterflies to visit. Butterflies help the environment by spreading pollen from plant to plant, plus you'll enjoy watching them flutter around. See how many types you can spot, and then try building your own LEGO versions.

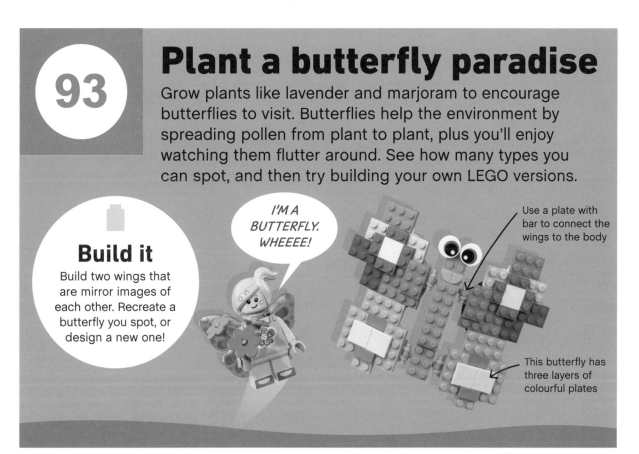

Build it

Build two wings that are mirror images of each other. Recreate a butterfly you spot, or design a new one!

I'M A BUTTERFLY. WHEEEE!

Use a plate with bar to connect the wings to the body

This butterfly has three layers of colourful plates

94 And breeeeathe!

Breathe yourself calm when things get too much. Breathe in deeply through your nose for a count of four, hold your breath for four, and then breathe out deeply through your mouth for four. Just imagine you're smelling a flower and then blowing out candles on a cake!

Be kind to furry friends

Owning a pet is a lot of fun, but it's a big responsibility too. Pets need to be fed, watered, taken for walks or exercise, groomed, and cleaned out regularly. Before getting a pet, decide as a family who will be responsible for each task. In the meantime, have fun building your dream pet with LEGO bricks – or you could just stick with your LEGO version!

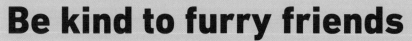

Sloped bricks for long bunny ears

IS IT TIME FOR WALKIES?

Long plates look like dog's droopy ears

WHAT'S ON THE MENU TODAY?

You don't have to choose realistic colours for your dream pet!

Antenna elements make cute cat whiskers

Build it

Once you've built your adorable animal, why not build a bed and food bowl too? What else will it need?

96

Take a shower challenge

Having a shower instead of a bath uses much less water – and shorter showers are even better! Set a timer and take on a family challenge to see who can take the shortest shower while still getting clean. Start scrubbing!

I'M THE WINNER TODAY, DUCKY!

97

Look around you!

Look up, down, and all around, and seek out the things that make you happy. What made you smile today? A squirrel running up a tree? Eating a delicious ice cream? Spotting a huge sunflower? Build what made you happy.

I'M VERY HAPPY TO SERVE YOU

Build it

Think about how you could use your bricks in different ways. Goblets make cool ice-cream cones.

Ice-cream van has headlights, a bumper, and a very important serving hatch

Create a "tower of change"

Keep track of your good deeds and achievements. Stack a LEGO brick on top of another for every change you make, every brave act, and every kind thing you do – and watch your "tower of change" grow!

Build it

2x4 bricks make sturdy towers. Add minifigures and accessories as a reminder of what you have achieved.

ONE LITTLE CHANGE...

...LEADS TO ANOTHER!

Helped out a friend? Stack a brick! →

Been brave and joined a new dance class? Add a dancer minifigure

Made a real effort to recycle? Stack a brick! ↙

If your tower gets too tall and unwieldy, start another one! →

Done something to help animals? Add an animal figure to a brick

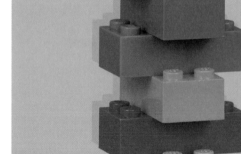

Spread some cheer

Be a ray of sunshine by spreading some happiness wherever you go. A little kindness can make a big difference to the people around you. Try to do something kind every day. What about starting with a cheery "good morning!" to someone you wouldn't usually greet?

Over to you!

Can you think of any other ways you could make a difference to the world around you? Whether it's caring for others, yourself, or the planet – small changes can make a BIG difference.

Checklist

Why not tick off the changes you make, the activities you complete, and the random acts of kindness you perform? Seeing the ticks will make you feel good about everything you are doing.

1 Offer a hug
2 Pick up a friendship
3 Boost positivity
4 Ready, steady, grow...
5 Get moving!
6 Give a thank-you card
7 Save your pennies
8 Make someone laugh
9 Be animal aware
10 Become a tidying whizz

11 Celebrate differences
12 Be a litter champion
13 Share your skills
14 Eat a rainbow
15 Create a family game
16 Talk to the new kid
17 Be a food-waste hero
18 3, 2, 1... run!
19 Go on a bug hunt
20 Give toys a new home

21 Discover your history
22 Love yourself
23 Sing for joy
24 Host an awards night
25 Go on a pet adventure
26 Share it!
27 Be kind online
28 Top a chore chart
29 Bring the birthday joy
30 Help a classmate

31 Offer your seat
32 Start a chain of creativity
33 Say cheese!
34 Be the news
35 Lights out
36 Solve it!
37 Bee friendly
38 Welcome everyone
39 Have your say
40 Step into their shoes

41 Be brave
42 Swap it!
43 Make your school sparkle
44 Be a chef
45 Celebrate you!
46 Hunt for rainbows
47 Become a team player
48 Borrow kindly
49 Turn off the tap
50 Tell a LEGO® tale

- [ ] **51** Be awesome and recycle
- [ ] **52** Make someone feel great
- [ ] **53** Unplug it!
- [ ] **54** Celebrate where you live
- [ ] **55** Go bird-watching
- [ ] **56** Look on the bright side
- [ ] **57** Befriend an elderly person
- [ ] **58** Have sweet dreams
- [ ] **59** Be fair!
- [ ] **60** Start a club

- [ ] **81** Listen to others
- [ ] **82** Volunteer at school
- [ ] **83** Give a thoughtful gift
- [ ] **84** Meet new critters
- [ ] **85** Start a special book club
- [ ] **86** Buy local
- [ ] **87** Explore the world
- [ ] **88** Give a helping hand
- [ ] **89** Save paper
- [ ] **90** Celebrate the little things

- [ ] **61** Surprise a pal
- [ ] **62** Celebrate heroes
- [ ] **63** Build together
- [ ] **64** Host a book swap
- [ ] **65** Stand up for what's right
- [ ] **66** Thank your teacher
- [ ] **67** Be a good neighbour
- [ ] **68** Say no to rubbish
- [ ] **69** Start a worm farm
- [ ] **70** Be their biggest fan

- [ ] **91** Be kind to yourself
- [ ] **92** Do something you love every day
- [ ] **93** Plant a butterfly paradise
- [ ] **94** And breeeeathe!
- [ ] **95** Be kind to furry friends
- [ ] **96** Take a shower challenge
- [ ] **97** Look around you!
- [ ] **98** Create a "tower of change"
- [ ] **99** Spread some cheer
- [ ] **100** Over to you!

- [ ] **71** Wish them well
- [ ] **72** Respect the rules
- [ ] **73** Focus your mind
- [ ] **74** Be kind, tidy!
- [ ] **75** Start a "library of things"
- [ ] **76** Be a kindness detective
- [ ] **77** Get outdoors!
- [ ] **78** Treat someone
- [ ] **79** Grow vegetables
- [ ] **80** Read all about it!

WHAT DID YOU DO TODAY?

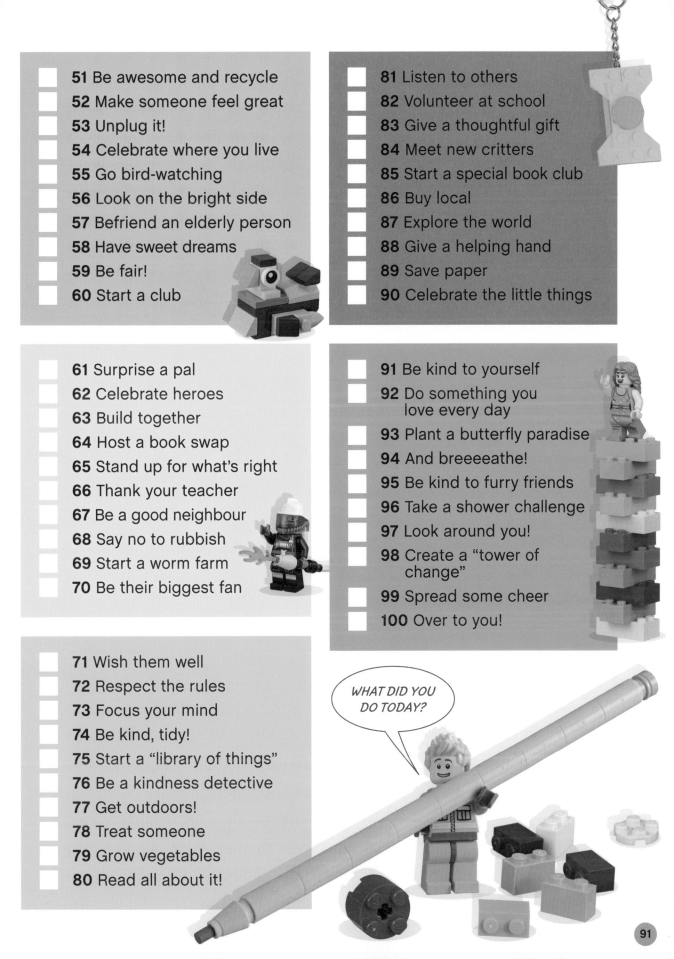

DK | Penguin Random House

Senior Editor Helen Murray
Project Art Editor Sam Bartlett
Designer James McKeag
Production Editor Siu Yin Chan
Senior Production Controller Lloyd Robertson
Managing Editor Paula Regan
Managing Art Editor Jo Connor
Publisher Julie Ferris
Art Director Lisa Lanzarini
Publishing Director Mark Searle

Photography Gary Ombler

Inspirational LEGO models built by:
Sebastiaan Arts, Stephen Berry, Jason Briscoe, Stuart Crawshaw, Emily Corl, Yvonne Doyle, Naomi Farr, Alice Finch, Rod Gillies, Tim Goddard, Kevin Hall, Deborah Higdon, Tim Johnson, Tori Kosara, Barney Main, Drew Maughan, James McKeag, Pete Reid, Duncan Titmarsh, and Andrew Walker.

Dorling Kindersley would like to thank Randi K. Sørensen, Heidi K. Jensen, Robin James Pearson, Paul Hansford, Martin Leighton Lindhardt, Kristofer Alan Crockett, Mathew Steven Boyle, Mette Buchbjerg, Ryan Greenwood, Mari-Louise Jonsson, Monika Lütke-Daldrup, and Andrea Du Rietz at the LEGO Group; Julia March and Rosie Peet for additional text and editorial assistance; Lauren Adams for design assistance.

First published in Great Britain in 2020 by Dorling Kindersley Limited
One Embassy Gardens, 8 Viaduct Gardens, London SW11 7BW

A Penguin Random House Company
10 9 8 7 6 5 4 3 2 1
001-320966-OCT/2020

Manufactured by Dorling Kindersley
One Embassy Gardens, 8 Viaduct Gardens, London SW11 7BW under licence from the LEGO Group.

A CIP catalogue record for this book is available from the British Library.

ISBN: 978-0-24145-821-1

Printed in China

For the curious

www.dk.com
www.LEGO.com